DART AND DIVE

ACROSS THE

REEF

To all the people working hard to save
our reefs, thank you for everything you do.

To my editors Anna Ridley and Sara Forster,
thank you for all your support.

VASSILIKI TZOMAKA

DART AND DIVE
ACROSS THE
REEF

Life in the world's busiest reefs

CONTENTS

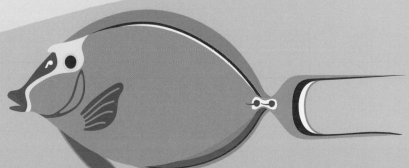

WHAT IS A REEF?

Rainforests of the sea

Coral reefs are often called the rainforests of the sea because they provide shelter to many sea animals and plants. They form around rocks and land formations, such as islands, over hundreds of years.

Although reefs cover less than 1% of the ocean floor, they are home to 25% of all known marine species and provide millions of humans with food and protection from rising sea levels and storms.

This book explores the incredible wildlife that exists in our reefs and explains why we need to keep these extraordinary places safe.

Types of tropical reefs

There are three main types of tropical reefs and each has a very different shape.

Fringing reefs grow very close to the shoreline and in some cases can be attached to land.

Barrier reefs grow further from the shore and have water between the reef and land.

Atoll reefs are ring shaped, with a lagoon in the center. They are formed when the land they are attached to sinks, leaving behind just the coral reef.

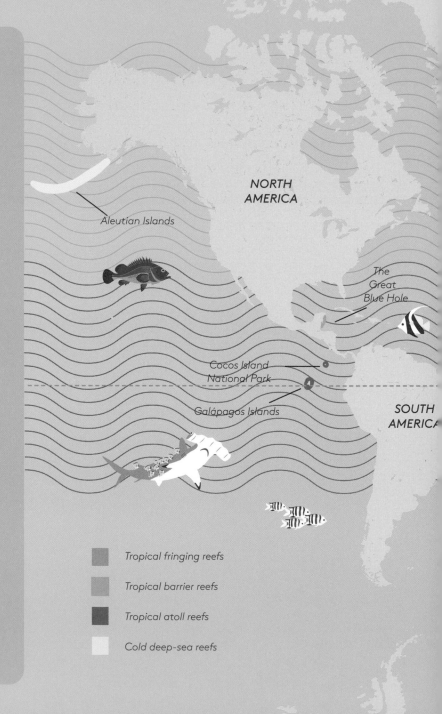

NORTH AMERICA

Aleutian Islands

The Great Blue Hole

Cocos Island National Park

Galápagos Islands

SOUTH AMERICA

Tropical fringing reefs

Tropical barrier reefs

Tropical atoll reefs

Cold deep-sea reefs

Both tropical and cold

Reefs found close to the equator, where the sea is warm, are known as tropical reefs. They form near land and near the surface of the sea.

Cold water reefs are found in much deeper waters. It is much harder for scientists to access deep-sea reefs so we are still discovering more about life here.

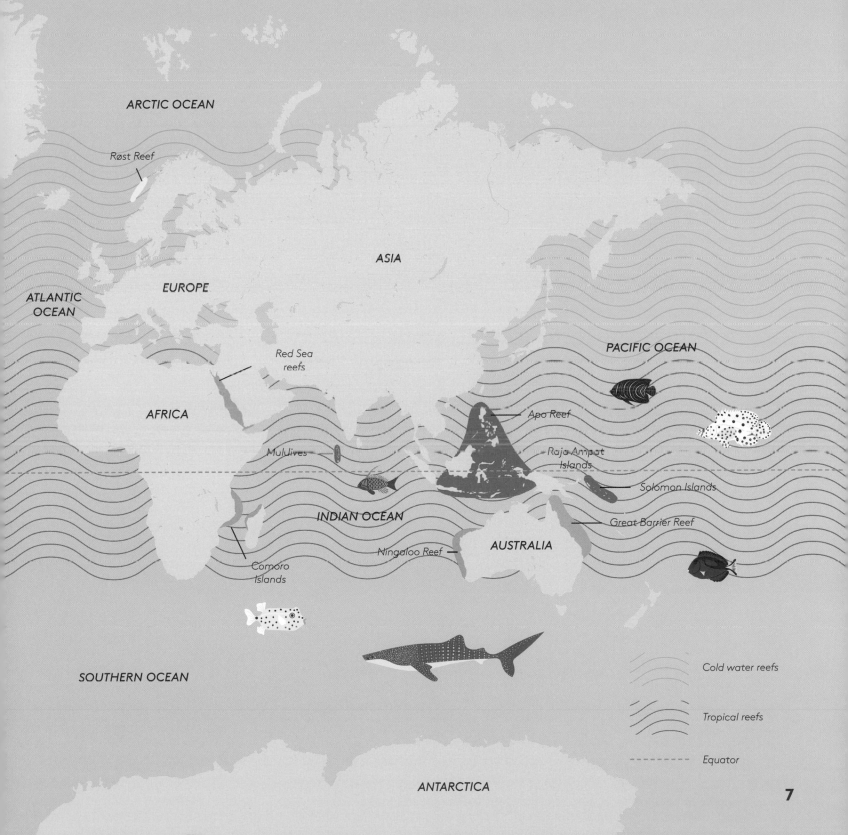

ARCTIC OCEAN

Røst Reef

ASIA

EUROPE

ATLANTIC
OCEAN

PACIFIC OCEAN

Red Sea
reefs

AFRICA

Apo Reef

Maldives

Raja Ampat
Islands

Solomon Islands

INDIAN OCEAN

Great Barrier Reef

Ningaloo Reef

AUSTRALIA

Comoro
Islands

SOUTHERN OCEAN

Cold water reefs

Tropical reefs

- - - - - - - Equator

ANTARCTICA

CORALS
Important creatures

Corals are often mistaken for plants or rocks, but they are actually made up of hundreds of thousands of tiny living animals called polyps. There are many different types of coral which grow in a wide variety of colors, shapes and sizes. When the polyps die they become hard and new polyps grow on top of them—that is how the coral reef slowly grows bigger over time.

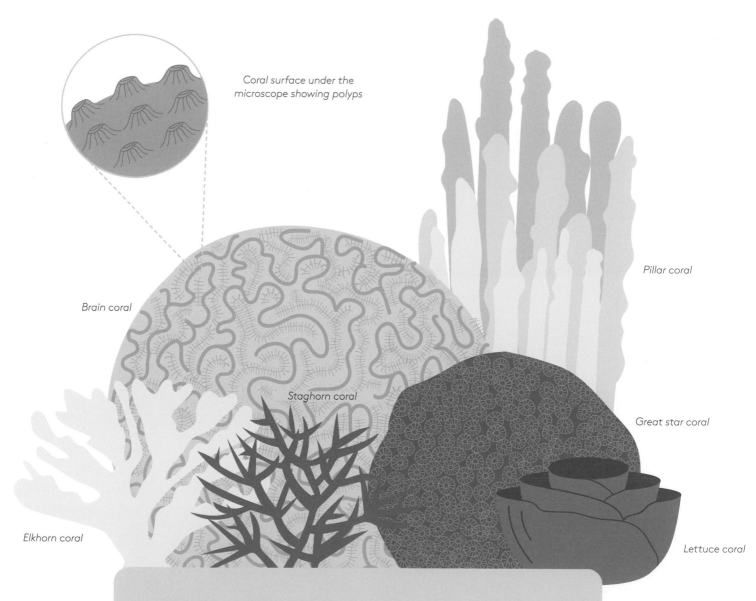

Coral surface under the microscope showing polyps

Pillar coral

Brain coral

Staghorn coral

Great star coral

Elkhorn coral

Lettuce coral

Hard corals

Hard corals are the building blocks of the reef. They grow together in large groups in a variety of shapes and sizes. Some are round while others are pointy and branching. The shape of a coral reef often depends on its location. Hard corals with rounded shapes, like brain coral, are found on reefs with strong waves. Pointed corals, like elkhorn or staghorn, grow on more sheltered reefs because their thin branches could be damaged or snapped off in the waves.

Soft corals

Unlike hard corals, soft corals do not have a solid skeleton. They are often mistaken for plants. Soft corals have no roots and sometimes sway in the water.

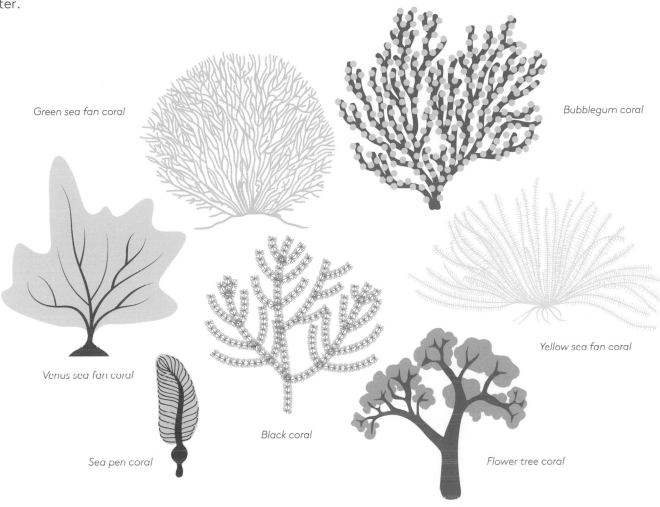

Green sea fan coral

Bubblegum coral

Venus sea fan coral

Yellow sea fan coral

Sea pen coral

Black coral

Flower tree coral

Polyps and plankton

Most polyps spend the day sleeping. When the sun goes down they wake up and stretch out their tentacles to snatch food that passes by. Their food, called plankton, is so tiny that we cannot see it without the help of a microscope.

Polyp asleep

Polyp awake

Plankton under the microscope

GREAT BARRIER REEF

A careful balance

The Great Barrier Reef off the coast of Australia is the largest coral reef in the world. It is so big that it can be seen from outer space! It is home to thousands of species, which are all on the look out for food. On a healthy reef, it is very important that there is a balance between predators and prey so that there is enough food for everyone.

The **tiger shark** is at the top of the food chain. It likes an easy meal so it will eat almost anything it finds. It locates its prey using special sensors in the skin near its nose.

The **emperor angelfish** has a strong bite and spends lots of its time grazing on algae, corals and sponges.

The **blue starfish** can grow to be 11.8 in wide. It makes a tasty meal for the **mantis shrimp**.

The **humphead wrasse** is an important predator on the reef because it eats venomous animals that feed on coral, like the crown-of-thorns starfish and the sea urchin.

The **blue tang** feeds on algae. This helps to keep the reef healthy, as it stops the algae from overgrowing and suffocating the coral.

Male lyretail anthias followed by females

Bannerfish

Lyretail anthias and **bannerfish** feed on plankton. They live and travel in large groups called schools.

Christmas tree worm

The **mantis shrimp** has very strong claws and can throw a good punch to protect itself. It eats small crustaceans and **Christmas tree worms**.

SOLOMON ISLANDS

Spots, stripes and other patterns

The Solomon Island reefs are made up of rocky corals, sandy patches, mangroves and lagoons. The closeness of these varied environments attracts many species, allowing scientists to observe the different ways that fish look, behave and communicate with each other.

The **yellow coris wrasse** has a spot on its back that looks like an eye. This helps to confuse its predators about which way the wrasse is swimming.

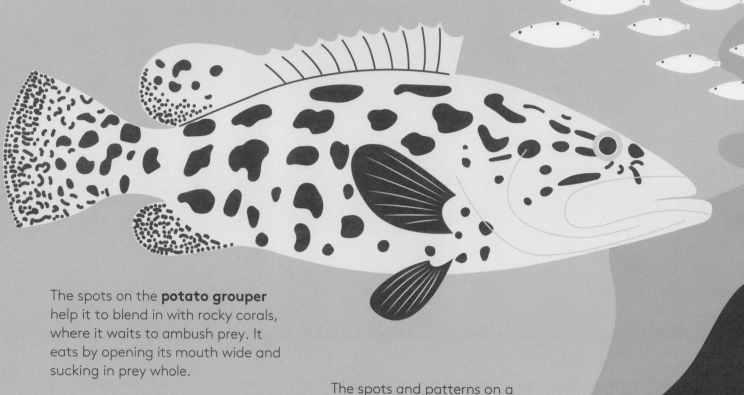

The spots on the **potato grouper** help it to blend in with rocky corals, where it waits to ambush prey. It eats by opening its mouth wide and sucking in prey whole.

The spots and patterns on a **clown triggerfish** help to confuse predators. From below, the white spots look like the surface of the water.

The **honeycomb grouper** gets its name from the hexagonal patterns on its scales. Its striking pattern helps it to blend in with bits of coral and the sandy seabed.

The banded stripes on the **moorish idol** help to dazzle and confuse predators. Unfortunately, these fish are very popular with aquarium keepers and often die in captivity.

The **banded sea krait** can be found in the sea and on land. Because its stripes are so uniform, predators can't work out which end its venomous bite is going to come from so they stay away.

The **humpback grouper** has a very unusual shape. The species is under threat of extinction because too many are being caught and eaten by humans.

The **tasselled wobbegong shark's** scale pattern makes it easy for it to hide near rocks and corals, waiting for its prey to pass by. When it is still, it is very hard to spot.

NIGHTTIME ON THE REEF

A midnight dive

Reefs remain busy when the sun goes down and the sea is in darkness. Nocturnal fish that have spent the day sleeping in caves or crevices come out to look for food. Daytime fish hide and get some rest. Sea creatures that are nocturnal usually have the ability to glow in the dark. They use this special trick to either attack prey or scare predators away.

The **longspine squirrelfish**, like most nocturnal fish, has large eyes that allow it to see better in the dark.

The **parrotfish** finds crevices to hide in when it is dark. It covers itself in a transparent cocoon to deter hungry predators while it sleeps.

The **emerald crab** comes out at night. It will eat almost anything it can get its claws on.

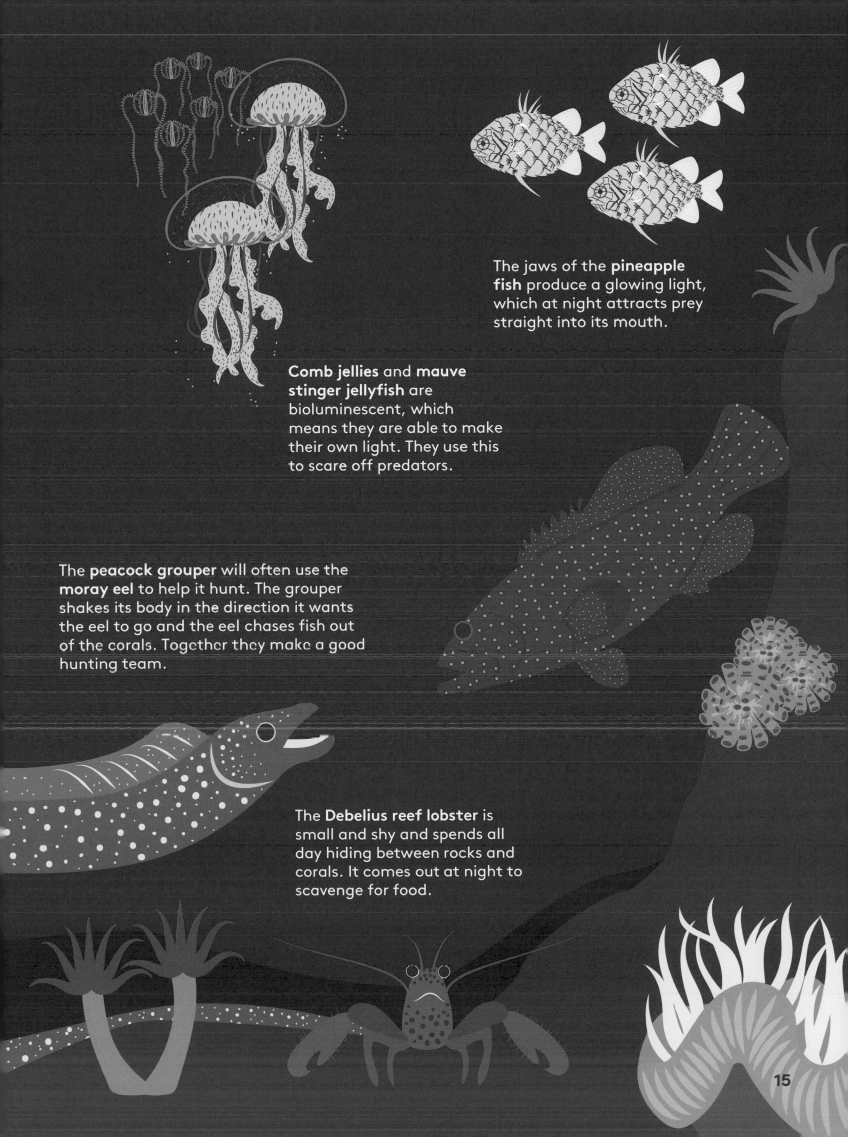

The jaws of the **pineapple fish** produce a glowing light, which at night attracts prey straight into its mouth.

Comb jellies and **mauve stinger jellyfish** are bioluminescent, which means they are able to make their own light. They use this to scare off predators.

The **peacock grouper** will often use the **moray eel** to help it hunt. The grouper shakes its body in the direction it wants the eel to go and the eel chases fish out of the corals. Together they make a good hunting team.

The **Debelius reef lobster** is small and shy and spends all day hiding between rocks and corals. It comes out at night to scavenge for food.

15

HAWKSBILL TURTLE

Long-distance traveler

The hawksbill turtle gets its name from the beak-like shape of its mouth. This sharp, narrow beak helps it to reach the sponges that it likes to eat, which grow in crevices on the reef. Even though the turtles are found in all tropical reefs and seas, they are endangered—humans hunt them for their beautifully patterned shells.

Dangerous dinners

As well as sponges, crustaceans and small fish, hawksbill turtles love to eat jellyfish.

Unfortunately, a floating plastic bag can look a lot like a jellyfish or algae to a turtle so they often end up eating plastic by mistake.

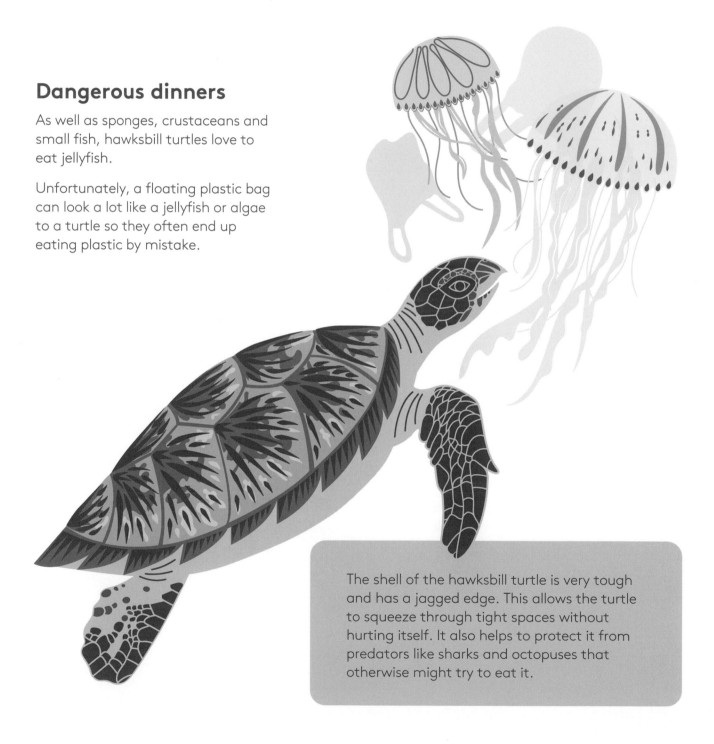

The shell of the hawksbill turtle is very tough and has a jagged edge. This allows the turtle to squeeze through tight spaces without hurting itself. It also helps to protect it from predators like sharks and octopuses that otherwise might try to eat it.

TURTLE NESTS

Every few years, female turtles will return to certain beaches at nighttime and dig a pit to lay and bury their eggs in.

After 40–80 days the eggs hatch.

The baby turtles dig their way out of the buried nest and make their way to the sea.

TYPES OF TURTLE

The hawksbill is one of seven types of turtle found in the world, nearly all of which are endangered.

1. Leatherback turtle

2. Loggerhead turtle

3. Green turtle

4. Flatback sea turtle

5. Hawksbill turtle

6. Olive Ridley turtle

7. Kemp's Ridley sea turtle

1.

2.

3.

4.

5.

6.

7.

RAJA AMPAT ISLANDS

Bursting with biodiversity

The Raja Ampat Islands in the Coral Triangle are some of the most biodiverse coral reef systems on the planet. Raja Ampat is home to over 1,300 species of coral reef fish and 600 species of hard corals. The area is particularly famous for its angelfish, with 86 of the 88 species in the world found here.

Two adult emperor angelfish followed by a school of juvenile emperor angelfish

Angelfish only live in groups when they are young and need protection from their parents. Once they grow up they like to live alone or in pairs.

Angelfish are not very strong swimmers so they stick to shallow parts of the reef where the sea currents are gentle. Here they can nibble on sponges, corals and small crustaceans.

Blue girdled angelfish

Regal angelfish

The flat shape of the angelfish means we can only see their colors and patterns from the side.

Juvenile semicircle angelfish

Juvenile blue girdled angelfish

Six bar angelfish

Blackstriped angelfish

Two-spined angelfish

APO REEF

Pretty in pink

Found at the top of the Coral Triangle, the Apo Reef in the Philippines is famous for its pink corals. Its shallow waters and lagoons make the perfect habitat for many different species. But where there are so many fish, there are also many predators, so species here have developed special ways of keeping out of harm's way.

The **yellowmargin triggerfish** has a hard, dorsal spine on the top of its head. It uses it to warn off predators and to wedge itself in place among the corals while it sleeps.

Spider decorator crab

Chocolate chip starfish

The **pygmy seahorse** is a tiny seahorse that only grows to 1.06 in tall. Seahorses can wrap their tails around corals or seaweed to help them stay in place in strong currents.

The **Muricella gorgonian coral** is a great hiding place for this seahorse family.

The **cone snail** tucks itself inside its hard shell to hide away from predators.

Miamira alleni nudibranch

The **coconut octopus** uses its tentacles to collect shells for covering up the entrance of its hideaway.

GALÁPAGOS ISLANDS

In and out the water

The Galápagos Islands are made up of a chain of submerged volcanoes 620 mi off the coast of Ecuador. Their remote position means that not all types of animals can reach them. Most of the mammals, reptiles and birds that live here have adapted to this secluded environment and get their food from the sea.

The **blue-footed booby** can dive into the sea from 100 ft high at speeds of up to 60 mph to hunt for fish. To attract a mate, the male takes large steps to show off its bright blue feet.

The **Galápagos penguin** stays close to the shore when searching for food. It must be careful of predators like sea lions and seals.

School of sardines

The **Galápagos sea lion** can stay underwater for up to 10 minutes and reach depths of nearly 2,000 ft. It swims up to 9.5 mi from the shore searching for **sardines** to eat but will also hunt fish that are found on the reefs.

Galápagos fur seals spend the daytime basking in the sun. At night they dive into the rocky reef to hunt for squid and krill, one of the larger species of plankton.

The flightless **Galápagos cormorant** can only be found on the shores of Fernandina and Isabela Islands. It dives into the sea and uses its sharp, hooked beak to catch eels and octopus to eat.

Galápagos cormorant

The **marine iguana** is the only lizard in the world that forages for food underwater. It removes salt from the seawater it drinks by sneezing it out through its nose.

The **red-lipped batfish** is a poor swimmer so it uses its fins to walk around.

The **Sally lightfoot crab** can jump from rock to rock and move quickly in any direction, both in and out of the water. It is excellent at scavenging for food.

COCOS ISLAND NATIONAL PARK

Underwater beauty salons

Hundreds of kilometers off the coast of Costa Rica, the steep coral slopes of the Cocos Islands make the perfect environment for cleaning stations. Here, small fish nibble at the dead skin of some of the ocean's top predators to give them a good clean. The little fish are safe cleaning the larger fish because they remove parasites, which helps keep the bigger fish healthy.

A **giant oceanic manta ray** glides into a station to have its gills cleaned by **barber fish** and **bluestreak cleaner wrasse**.

A group of **pilot fish** accompany the **whitetip reef shark** as it arrives from the wider ocean.

The hard shell of the **green turtle** provides a lot of food for **barber fish** and **king angelfish**. Sometimes this cleaning process can take up to an hour.

The **scalloped hammerhead shark** is a well-known visitor of these reefs. **Barber fish** gather around it to eat any parasites on the shark's skin.

Bluestreak cleaner wrasse are small and very common in cleaning stations. They get all their nutrition from cleaning the gills, teeth and skin of larger fish.

When it is busy, larger fish have to line up to be cleaned. Even the **whitetip reef shark**, a solitary fish that will eat anything, will wait patiently in line to be cleaned.

REEF BABIES

Born to be wild

Lots of fish reproduce by laying eggs but some species of sharks and rays give birth to live young. The reef is a dangerous place to be and some fish can't afford to stay and protect their eggs all day, so they have clever ways to keep their offspring safe.

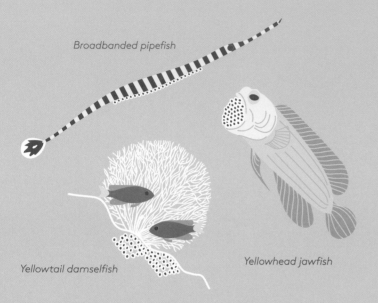

Broadbanded pipefish

Yellowtail damselfish

Yellowhead jawfish

Some fish, like the **yellowtail damselfish**, lay their eggs in nests that they fiercely guard but others protect their eggs by keeping them close to their bodies. The male **yellowhead jawfish** keeps its eggs in its mouth until they are ready to hatch. The **broadbanded pipefish** carries them along its belly on a special patch of skin.

Some juvenile fish, like the **French angelfish**, look nothing like their parents. Angelfish can be very territorial so scientists think the babies look different to stop other adult fish from chasing them away.

Blacktip reef sharks give birth to 2–4 babies at a time, called pups. The adult females gather in warm, shallow waters to give birth, where the pups will be safe from predators. The pups will stay together in large groups until they are big enough to head out to deeper water.

FRAGMENTATION

Some starfish have a very unusual ability —they can regrow their limbs. When they want to reproduce they divide themselves in half and begin to regrow their missing limbs. When the process is complete, there are two perfect starfish.

THE SLENDER SEAHORSE
A pocketful of miracles

The slender seahorse is found in many tropical reefs. Like all other seahorses, it is the males that give birth to babies. The female deposits her eggs into the male's pouch, who will look after the eggs for about 20 days until they are ready to hatch.

The male slender seahorse will give birth to around 700 babies. The babies are about 6 mm tall when they are born and as soon as they leave their father's pouch they are on their own. Those that survive to adulthood will grow to around 7 in.

ALEUTIAN ISLANDS

Keeping kelp alive

The shallow rock reefs found near the coasts of the Aleutian Islands in Alaska are covered in ribbon kelp forests. Kelp can grow to over 164 ft tall and helps reduce global warming because it absorbs carbon dioxide from the atmosphere, just like plants and trees on land do.

The **Pacific purple sea urchin** feeds on kelp and will eat it until it is all gone. The **sea otter** and **sunflower starfish** eat sea urchins so together they stop them from eating too much of the kelp forests.

COLD WATER FISH

On the menu

The coral reefs around the Aleutian Islands attract many species of cold water fish that are caught by humans for food. It is very important that we don't catch too many fish so that the carefully balanced food chain isn't disrupted.

The **Atka mackerel** grows very quickly. It travels in large schools to protect itself from bigger predators.

The **Pacific cod** swims in very large schools and can grow up to 5.9 ft long.

Golden king crab

Yelloweye rockfish

The **golden king crab** can live at depths of 2,360 ft. It lives close to coral reefs that provide plenty of food and hiding places.

The **Pacific halibut** can grow to be 6.5 ft long. It hides on the sea floor, only jumping out to catch passing prey.

The **yelloweye rockfish** can live to be 150 years old. Once it has chosen a rocky patch as its territory, it stays close to it for its entire life.

OVERFISHING

Some methods of fishing can be very destructive to marine ecosystems. By using **trawling nets**, fishermen catch species of fish that we don't always want to eat and the nets often destroy the seabed and coral reefs. That's why it is important to make sure the fish we eat is caught sustainably.

RØST REEF

Cold, ancient and undisturbed

The recently discovered Røst Reef in the Norwegian Sea is home to the largest lophelia coral forest in the world. The reef is located 985-1310 ft below sea level and the water is a chilly 36°F. All the animals that live here have adapted to living in the cold and dark water and have relied on the coral reef for food and shelter for thousands of years.

Lophelia coral grows very slowly because the coral doesn't receive any sunlight deep underwater. Groups of lophelia that reach 5 ft tall are thought to be over 250 years old.

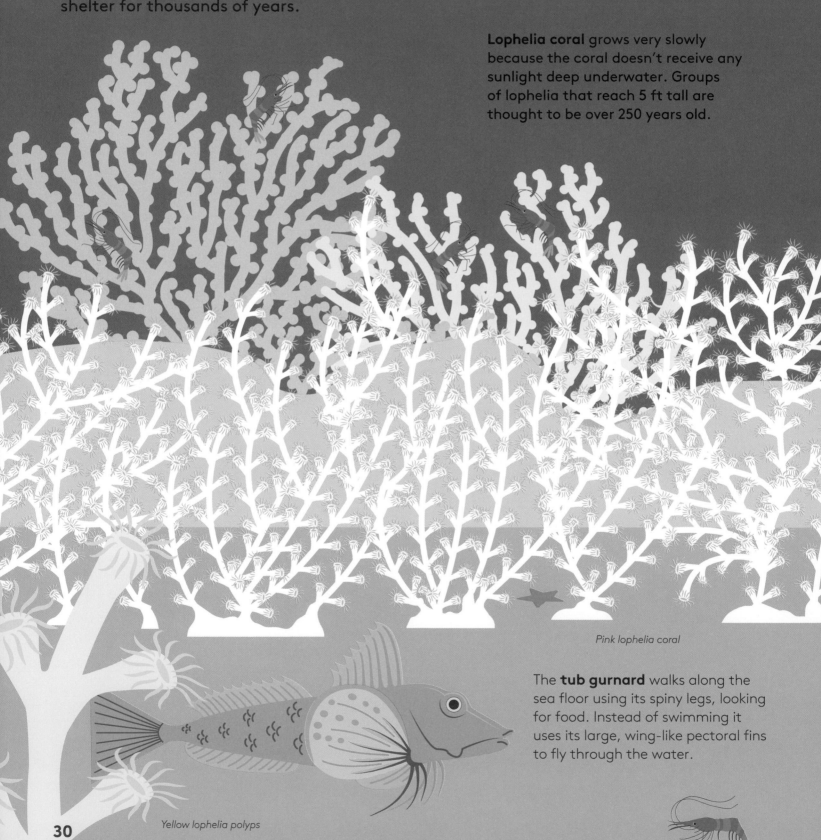

Pink lophelia coral

The **tub gurnard** walks along the sea floor using its spiny legs, looking for food. Instead of swimming it uses its large, wing-like pectoral fins to fly through the water.

Yellow lophelia polyps

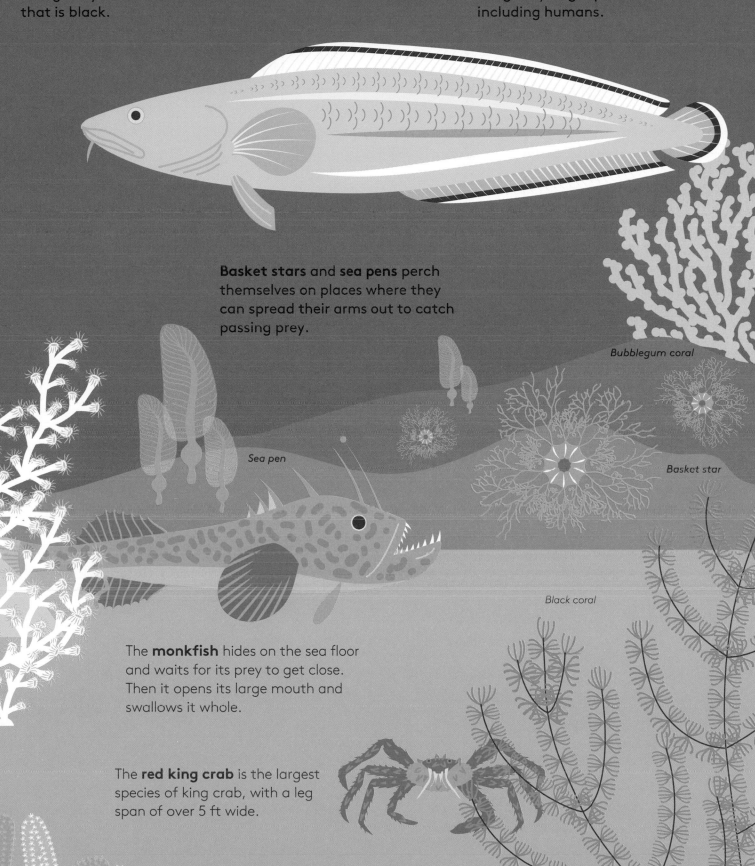

Bubblegum and black corals often grow near lophelia corals. Despite their name, black corals are bright orange or yellow—it's their skeleton that is black.

The cusk isn't a strong swimmer. It stays close to the sea floor to avoid being caught by larger predators, including humans.

Basket stars and sea pens perch themselves on places where they can spread their arms out to catch passing prey.

Bubblegum coral

Sea pen

Basket star

Black coral

The monkfish hides on the sea floor and waits for its prey to get close. Then it opens its large mouth and swallows it whole.

The red king crab is the largest species of king crab, with a leg span of over 5 ft wide.

Dead man's finger is a soft coral that looks like a furry gloved hand.

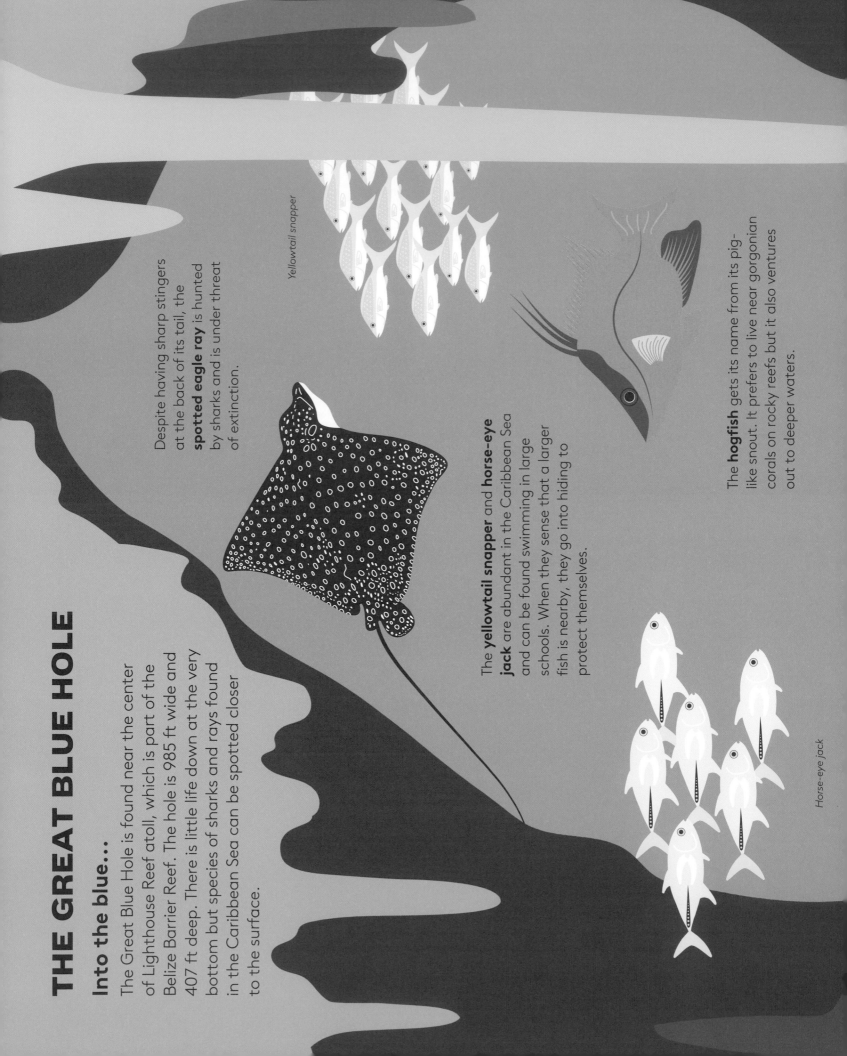

THE GREAT BLUE HOLE

Into the blue...

The Great Blue Hole is found near the center of Lighthouse Reef atoll, which is part of the Belize Barrier Reef. The hole is 985 ft wide and 407 ft deep. There is little life down at the very bottom but species of sharks and rays found in the Caribbean Sea can be spotted closer to the surface.

Despite having sharp stingers at the back of its tail, the **spotted eagle ray** is hunted by sharks and is under threat of extinction.

The **yellowtail snapper** and **horse-eye jack** are abundant in the Caribbean Sea and can be found swimming in large schools. When they sense that a larger fish is nearby, they go into hiding to protect themselves.

The **hogfish** gets its name from its pig-like snout. It prefers to live near gorgonian corals on rocky reefs but it also ventures out to deeper waters.

Yellowtail snapper

Horse-eye jack

The **great barracuda** is a fierce fish and a very fast swimmer. It snaps up smaller fish such as snappers and jacks with its strong jaws and sharp teeth.

The **Caribbean reef shark** likes to rest in the dark caves, giving the impression that it is asleep.

What is a blue hole?

The Great Blue Hole is a giant marine cavern. Scientists believe that thousands of years ago it was once a cave that gradually filled with sea water. That's why the blue hole has 40 ft long stalactites and stalagmites.

REEF INVERTEBRATES
Spineless but special

Marine invertebrates do not have spines so they have to rely on other mechanisms to support their bodies and move around. Some have hard shells that surround and protect them while others produce chemicals to survive.

Starfish, sea urchins and sea cucumbers are all **echinoderms.** Echinoderms move very slowly on the sea floor. Some echinoderms, like sea urchins, are covered in prickly spines to deter predators.

Jellyfish, corals and anemones are types of **cnidarians**. They have stinging cells on their tentacles or polyps that they use to catch food and to protect themselves against potential predators.

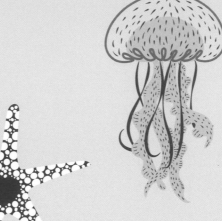

Mauve stinger jellyfish

Necklace starfish

Sea snails, nudibranchs and squid are types of **mollusks.** They have soft bodies but some species like oysters and clams live in a hard shell.

Red shrimp

Willan's chromodoris nudibranch

Lobsters, crabs and shrimps are all types of **crustaceans.** Crustaceans have a hard covering, or exoskeleton, that protects their soft bodies.

Sponges are an important part of coral reef ecosystems because they help to filter water. Sponges can grow quickly and live for hundreds of years. Some barrel sponges are big enough for a human to fit inside.

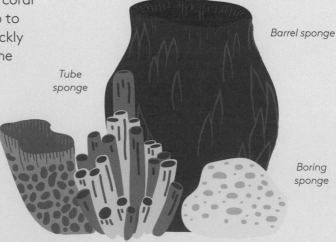

Barrel sponge

Tube sponge

Vase sponge

Boring sponge

REEF FISH

Take a look inside and out

All reef fish are vertebrates. This means that, like humans, they have a spine. Fish with spines made out of bone are called bony fish and fish with spines made out of cartilage are called cartilaginous fish. Most of the small fish that live on the reef are bony fish, but species like sharks and rays are cartilaginous.

The lateral line is made up of sensors that detect movements so fish know what is happening around them.

Fish eyes are rounded like marbles, which helps fish to see clearly underwater.

The scales form a protective armor

Dorsal fins

Ear

Nostril

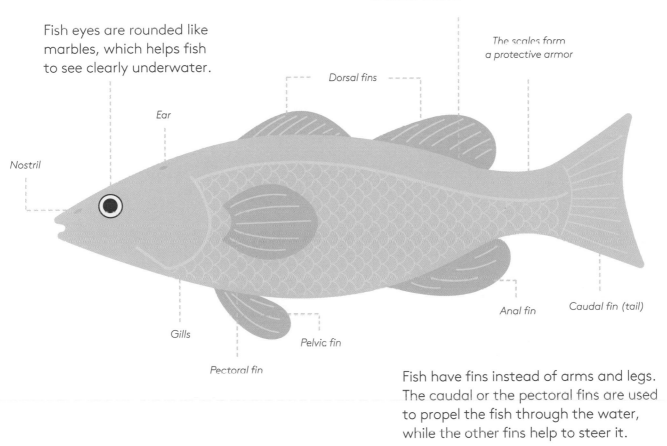

Gills

Pectoral fin

Pelvic fin

Anal fin

Caudal fin (tail)

Fish have fins instead of arms and legs. The caudal or the pectoral fins are used to propel the fish through the water, while the other fins help to steer it.

How do fish breathe and stay upright in the water?

To breath in the water, fish use their **gills**. These special organs filter the oxygen out of the water, just like our lungs filter the oxygen out of the air.

To stay upright in the water most bony fish have an organ called the **swim bladder**, which they fill with air depending on how deep they are swimming.

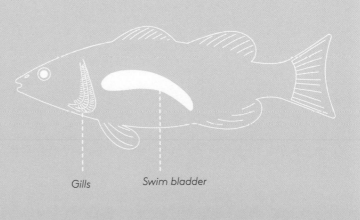

Gills

Swim bladder

RED SEA REEFS

Natural treasures

The coral reefs in the north of the Red Sea are home to some very unique species. The reefs are rich with marine life that can't be found anywhere else in the world. Luckily, the reefs are protected as part of Egypt's Ras Mohammed National Park.

The **Arabian surgeonfish** gets its name from its sharp, scalpel-like spine. When protecting its territory it can become quite aggressive, using its spine to attack its enemies.

The brightly colored **Red Sea flasher wrasse** spends all day looking for food. It is one of the first fish to hide when the sun goes down.

Red Sea garden eels live in the sandy seabed around reefs. As they wait for food to come to them, swaying with the current of the sea, they look like blades of grass.

Orange face butterflyfish travel in pairs looking for table coral to feast on. Once they find some they are very territorial.

Blue cheeked butterflyfish are gentle fish that not only travel in pairs, but stay together for life.

The **Klunzinger's wrasse** is only found in the Red Sea. It is a curious fish and will sometimes approach divers.

Rusty parrotfish get their name from the rust-like color of their bodies when they are very young. As they get older their scales change to a bright blue and green color.

SYMBIOSIS ON THE REEF
Unusual pairings

Some sea animals form close relationships with different species, often for food or protection. We call this relationship symbiosis. Sometimes both species benefit but other times one of the species can be harmed by the relationship.

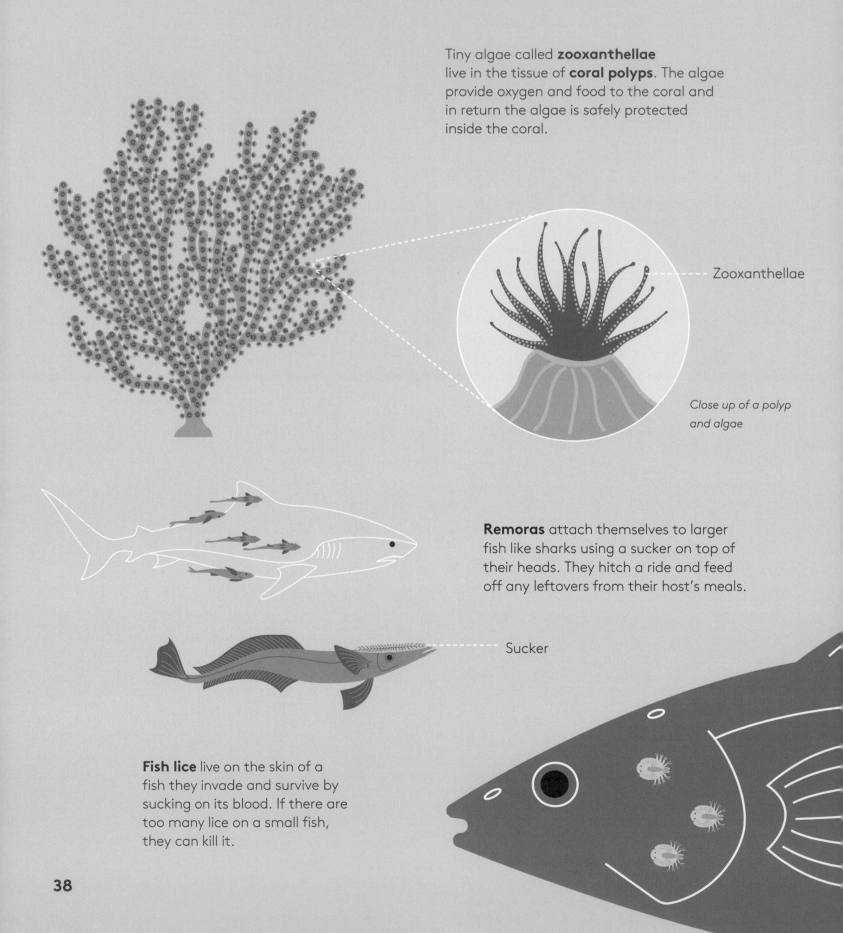

Tiny algae called **zooxanthellae** live in the tissue of **coral polyps**. The algae provide oxygen and food to the coral and in return the algae is safely protected inside the coral.

Zooxanthellae

Close up of a polyp and algae

Remoras attach themselves to larger fish like sharks using a sucker on top of their heads. They hitch a ride and feed off any leftovers from their host's meals.

Sucker

Fish lice live on the skin of a fish they invade and survive by sucking on its blood. If there are too many lice on a small fish, they can kill it.

THE CLOWN ANEMONEFISH

Home sweet home

The anemonefish (or clownfish) and the anemone have a special partnership. The anemonefish lives in the anemone and is provided with shelter and protection. In return, the anemonefish scares off any predatory fish and provides nutrients to the anemone.

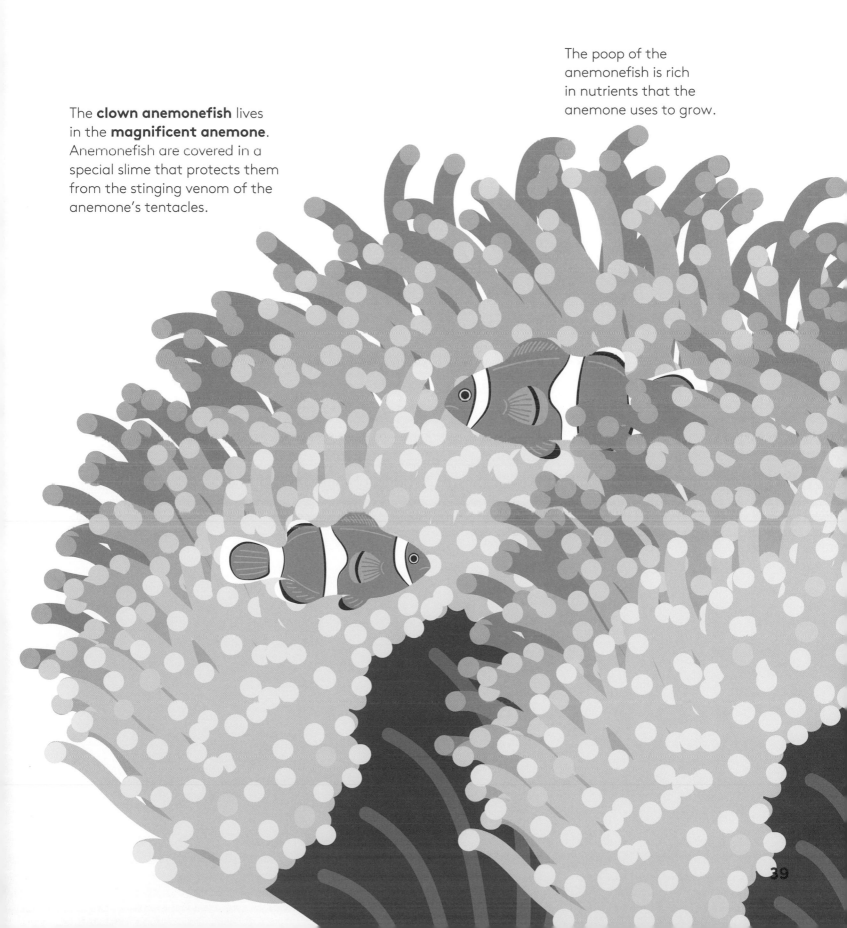

The poop of the anemonefish is rich in nutrients that the anemone uses to grow.

The **clown anemonefish** lives in the **magnificent anemone**. Anemonefish are covered in a special slime that protects them from the stinging venom of the anemone's tentacles.

COMORO ISLANDS

Reefs of hope

The pristine volcanic reefs of the Mozambique Channel are rich in marine life. Gorgonian corals arch over the sandy bottom, attracting many fish from the Indian Ocean. Scientists are investigating why the corals here are less sensitive to climate change, in the hope that they will find more ways to keep marine life safe.

Sailfin tangs are one of the largest tangs. Their bright colors fade to brown when they are feeling threatened.

The **yellow teardrop butterflyfish** gets its name from the black teardrop shape on its back. Like other butterflyfish they are very flat so they can swim in and out of the corals.

The **Zulu snakelet** likes to stick close to the seabed, where it can blend in and hide while looking for food. It is only found in a small area of the Indian Ocean.

Male and female **African pencil wrasse** look very different. The males are more colorful and larger than the smaller, pink-colored females.

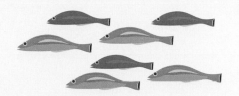

The skin of the **goldribbon grouper** contains a bitter toxin that it releases when scared. Its yellow stripe is a warning sign to predators that it won't be tasty.

The **yellow boxfish's** bright color warns any predators that it can release toxins when feeling threatened.

The **elegant unicornfish** has two sharp red blades that stick out near its tail which help to protect it from predators.

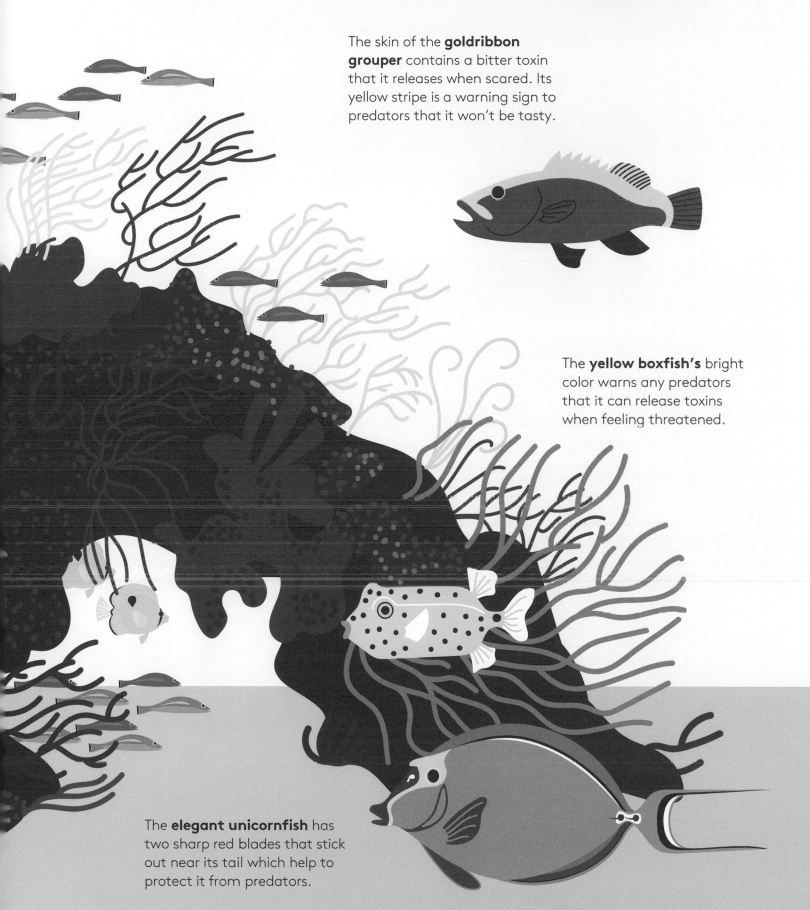

ATOLLS OF THE MALDIVES

Sociable or solitary

The Maldives are made up of a chain of 26 natural atolls and hundreds of small islands. Atolls are created when a volcano in the ocean erupts and slowly sinks into the sea over millions of years. The abundance of fish here makes it possible for us to spot which species like to travel in large groups and which prefer to hang out on their own.

The **gold ring bristletooth** has bristle-like teeth that scrape and sift algae from rocks and sand. Its body becomes darker as it gets older, turning from pink to blue.

The **bluespotted cornetfish** has a smooth scaleless body and prefers to live alone. It uses its long snout to suck up small fish from the seabed.

The **lagoon triggerfish** likes to keep its own company and will defend its territory fiercely. Some individuals have been observed defending the same territory for over 8 years.

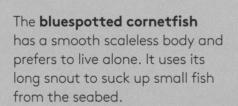

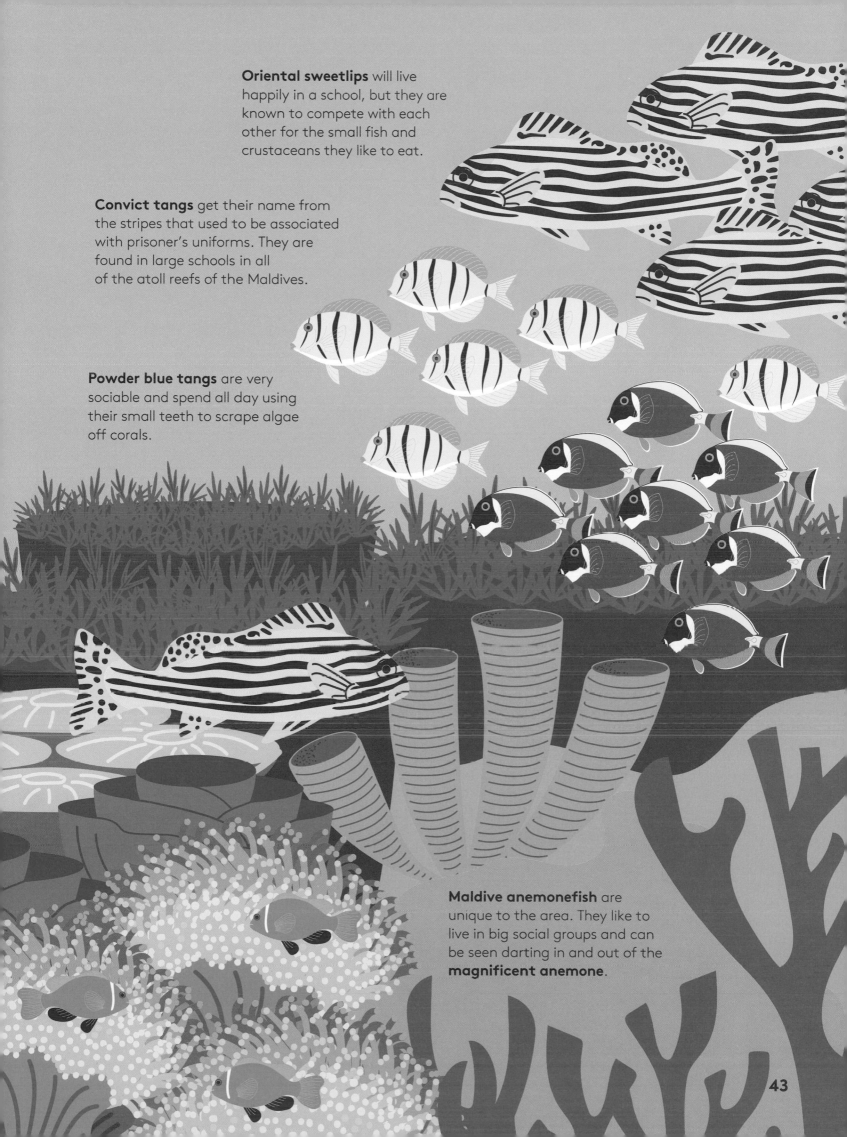

Oriental sweetlips will live happily in a school, but they are known to compete with each other for the small fish and crustaceans they like to eat.

Convict tangs get their name from the stripes that used to be associated with prisoner's uniforms. They are found in large schools in all of the atoll reefs of the Maldives.

Powder blue tangs are very sociable and spend all day using their small teeth to scrape algae off corals.

Maldive anemonefish are unique to the area. They like to live in big social groups and can be seen darting in and out of the **magnificent anemone**.

43

DEADLY CREATURES

Watch out

Many species of fish need to be able to defend themselves from predators on the reef. Some fish carry venom that they inject into predators through bites or stings. Other species are brightly colored, which warns predators that if they eat them, they will be poisoned.

The bright stripes on a **lion fish** act as a warning sign to predators that it is packed full of venom.

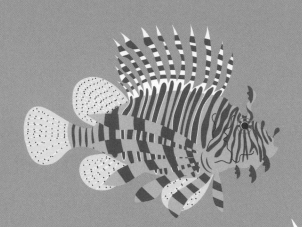

The **blowfish** swallows water, swelling up to twice its width so it is harder for predators to try to eat it. As some of its organs are poisonous it can paralyze the animals that do manage to eat it.

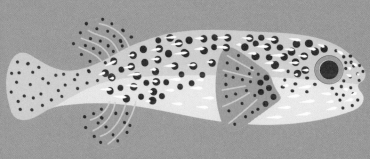

The bright spots on the **blue-ringed octopus** warn predators to stay away as the tiny octopus has a very venomous bite.

The **stone fish** is the most venomous fish in the world. It can sting predators like rays with its dorsal spines. It is excellent at hiding among rocky corals on the bottom of the reef floor.

DEFENSE MECHANISMS

Staying extra safe

Not all sea creatures can rely on poison or venom to defend themselves so they have developed special abilities that allow them to hide, protect themselves or have time to escape.

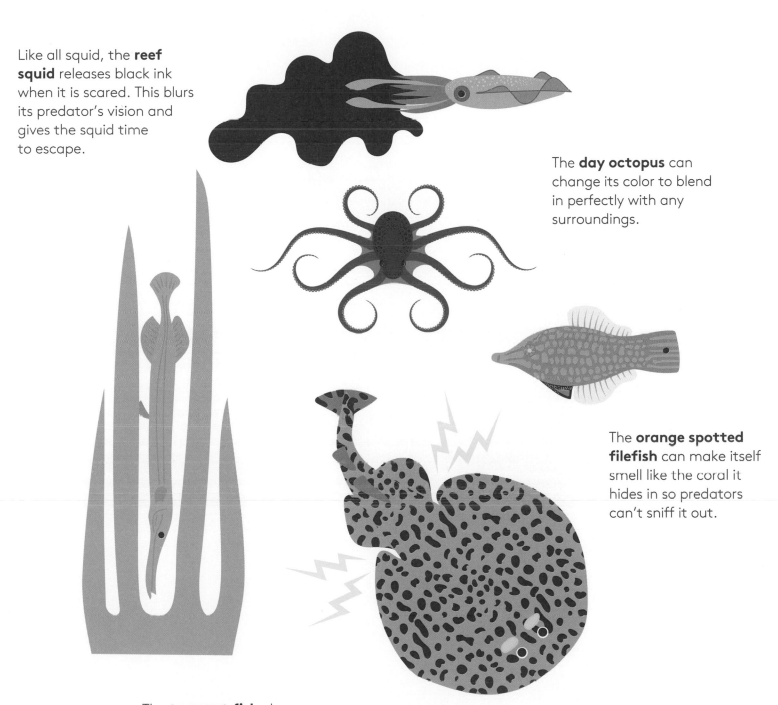

Like all squid, the **reef squid** releases black ink when it is scared. This blurs its predator's vision and gives the squid time to escape.

The **day octopus** can change its color to blend in perfectly with any surroundings.

The **orange spotted filefish** can make itself smell like the coral it hides in so predators can't sniff it out.

The **trumpet fish** changes color and floats vertically, which makes it look just like a piece of seaweed.

The **electric ray** produces an electric current that shocks its predators if they get too close.

NOISE ON THE REEF

Signs of a healthy reef

A healthy coral reef is one of the noisiest places on Earth. Marine animals make all sorts of different noises to communicate with each other. Some make sounds to warn each other of danger and others use noise to attract the attention of a potential mate. A noisy reef will also attract more species as they can follow the sounds till they find the reef.

The **big-belly seahorse** clicks, growls and tosses its head to communicate with other seahorses around it when foraging for food.

The **splendid toadfish** makes grunting sounds to alert others of danger, like if they spot predators like dolphins nearby.

Yellowfin anemonefish make chirping and popping sounds. They are also good at making a noise by gnashing their teeth to scare predators away.

46

Haddon's sea anemone

The **gulf corvina** is the noisiest reef fish of them all. It uses its swim bladder as a drum to attract other females and makes a sound that is as loud as a jet engine.

Blue striped grunts make a grunting noise by grinding their teeth together.

Blackbar soldierfish come out to hunt at night. They make grunting and clicking noises if they feel stressed, which warns their group of danger.

When the **pistol shrimp** punches its powerful claw, it produces air bubbles that stun its prey. This makes a bang louder than a gun being fired.

The **blue tuxedo sea urchin** has very large teeth that make a loud noise when it scrapes algae off rocks and corals.

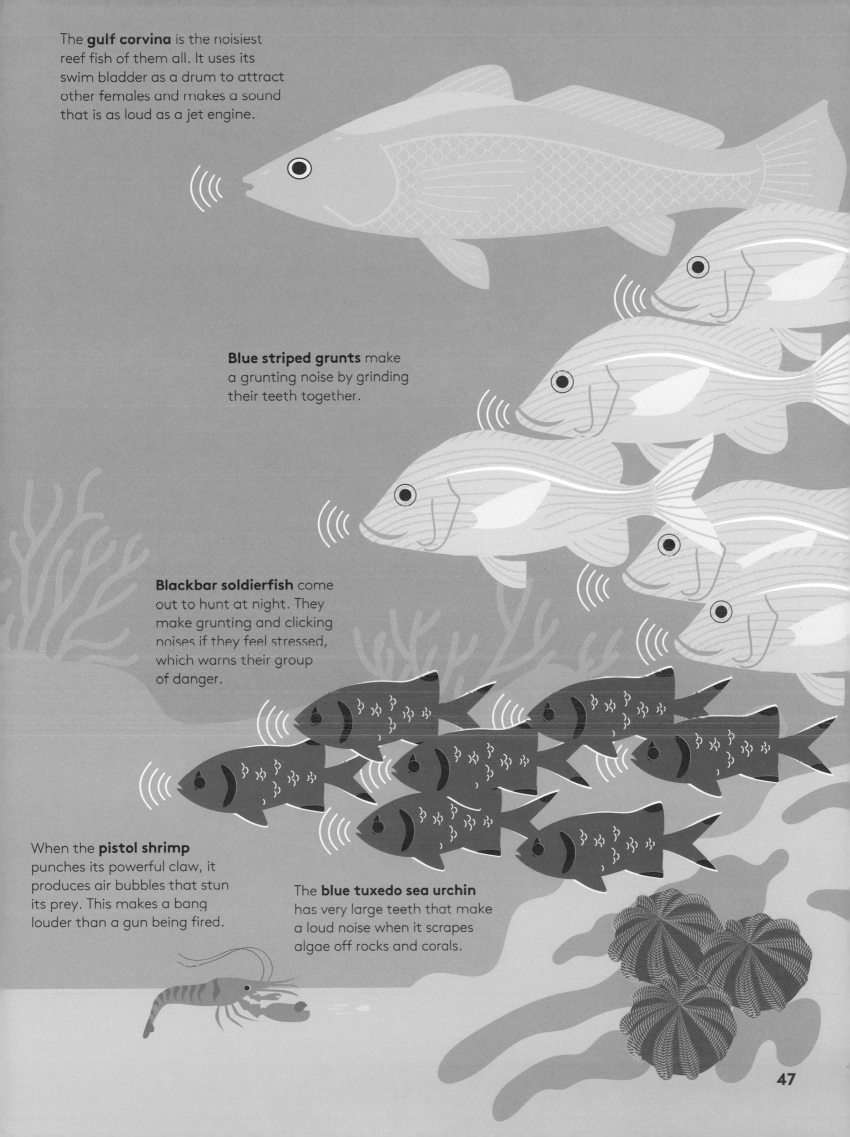

NINGALOO REEF

Playing in the big leagues

Ningaloo Reef is the largest fringing reef in the world. It stretches for 160 mi along the western coast of Australia. The water around the reef is warm and shallow but the seabed quickly drops away, allowing larger species that live in deeper waters to come close to the reef.

The **spinner dolphin** gets its name from the spinning acrobatics it performs when coming out of the water. They can be seen in pods of up to 200 swimming past the reef.

The **African pompano** is a large fish that visits the reef to feed on the many crustaceans and small fish found here.

Seagrass grows in the water sheltered by the reef. The **dugong** spends most of its time grazing on seagrass. It can stay underwater for up to 6 minutes before needing to surface to take a breath.

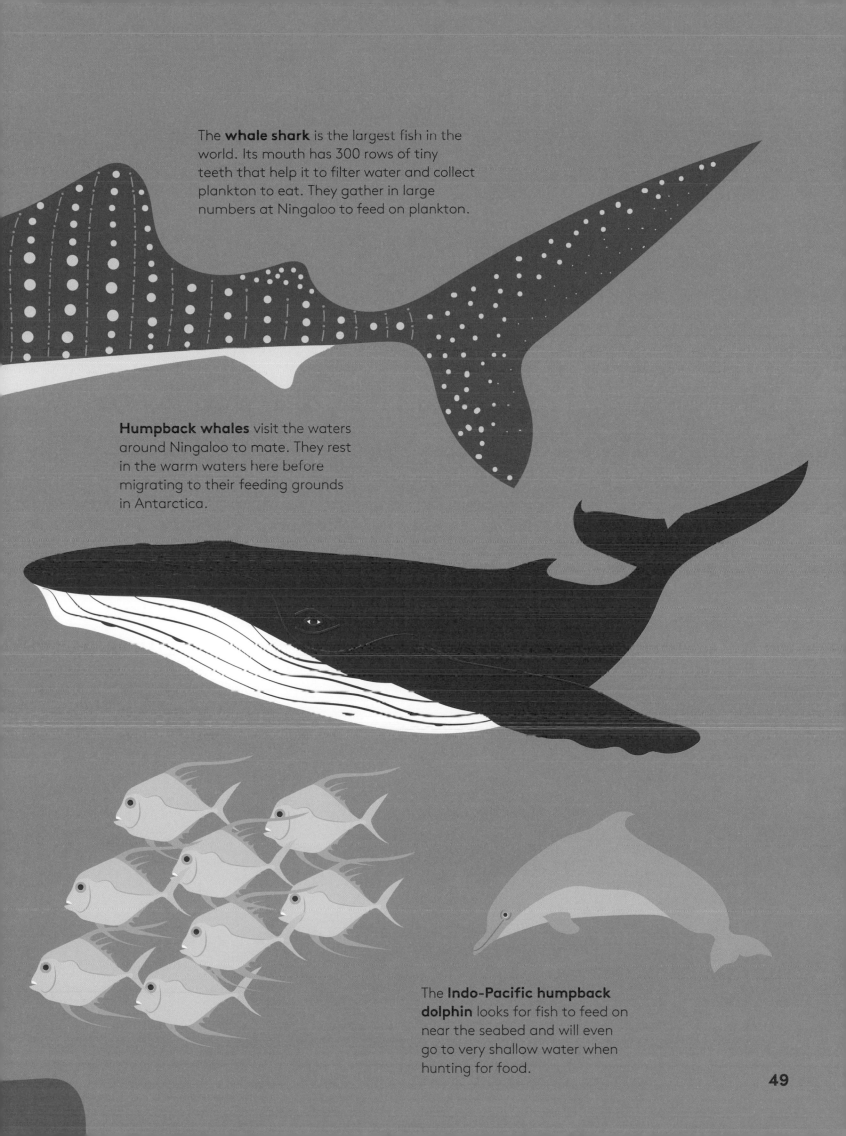

The **whale shark** is the largest fish in the world. Its mouth has 300 rows of tiny teeth that help it to filter water and collect plankton to eat. They gather in large numbers at Ningaloo to feed on plankton.

Humpback whales visit the waters around Ningaloo to mate. They rest in the warm waters here before migrating to their feeding grounds in Antarctica.

The **Indo-Pacific humpback dolphin** looks for fish to feed on near the seabed and will even go to very shallow water when hunting for food.

REEFS AT RISK

The way we live

Many of our activities on land, sometimes quite far from coral reefs, can cause a lot of harm to their delicate ecosystems.

Global warming

Most of the energy we use for heating, transportation and manufacturing comes from burning fossil fuels. This produces carbon dioxide (CO_2), a gas that escapes into the atmosphere. Trees normally absorb this gas to grow, but we are making too much of it, and this has resulted in a phenomenon called global warming. Global warming is making our seas warmer, which stresses the corals, putting the whole reef ecosystem at risk.

CO_2

CO_2

CO_2

Sedimentation

Deforestation and too much farming can loosen the earth so much that it slides into the sea and smothers corals.

Animals covered in sedimentation

Coral bleaching

Warmer sea temperatures can make coral stressed. When coral is stressed, it expels the zooxanthellae that live inside it. Without the zooxanthellae, the coral loses its color. This is known as coral bleaching. Corals can survive like this for some time but unless the zooxanthellae return, they are at risk of dying.

Polluting plastic

Unfortunately, most plastic does not get recycled and ends up in the sea. As it floats around, many sea animals often get trapped in it or swallow it.

Some plastic eventually breaks down into tiny pieces, known as **microplastics**. Although these can't be seen, they can still become trapped in gills and stomachs and make sea animals very sick.

Too much tourism

Visiting coral reefs is an amazing experience but when too many people visit and are careless, it causes problems. When an area becomes too busy, problems like garbage, stress to wildlife and damage to coral from people touching or standing on it can start to happen.

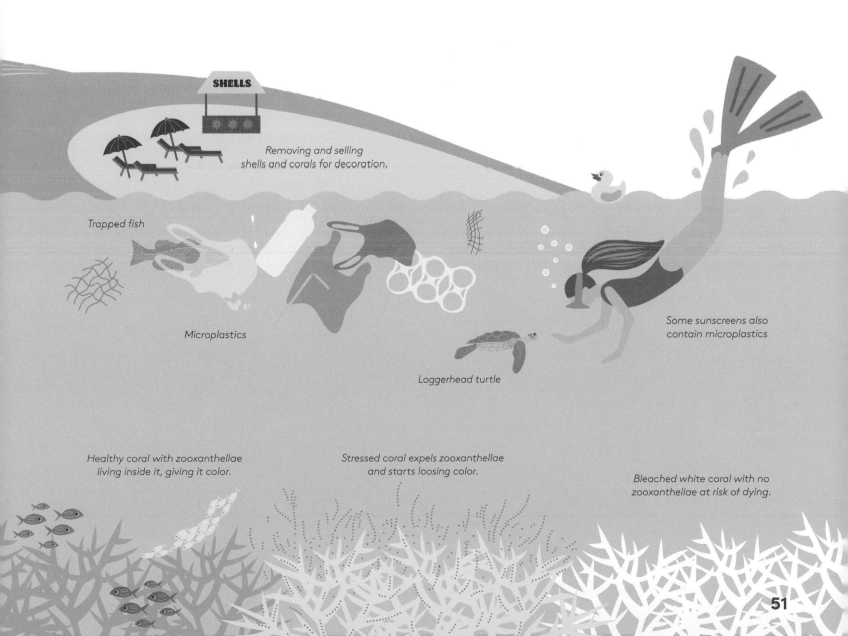

SHELLS

Removing and selling shells and corals for decoration.

Trapped fish

Microplastics

Loggerhead turtle

Some sunscreens also contain microplastics

Healthy coral with zooxanthellae living inside it, giving it color.

Stressed coral expels zooxanthellae and starts loosing color.

Bleached white coral with no zooxanthellae at risk of dying.

SAVING THE SEAS

Thinking ahead

Saving our reefs from coral bleaching is very important. Thinking about how we live and use energy and what we can do to produce less carbon dioxide, can make a big difference to our planet and its reefs.

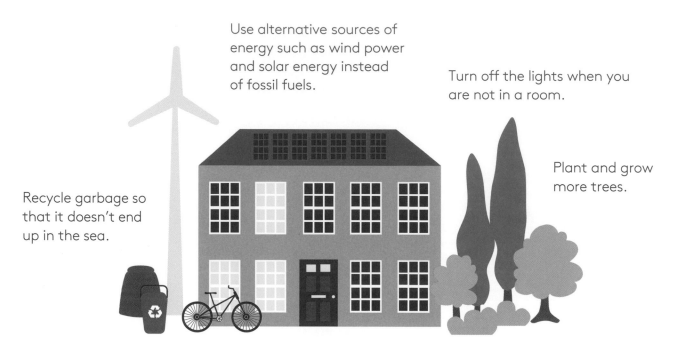

Use alternative sources of energy such as wind power and solar energy instead of fossil fuels.

Turn off the lights when you are not in a room.

Recycle garbage so that it doesn't end up in the sea.

Plant and grow more trees.

Bike or walk when possible.

How long will it take to decompose?

Knowing how long it takes for something we have used to be absorbed by the Earth can help us make better shopping choices and live more sustainably.

Fishing net
600 years

Plastic bottles
400 years

Tin cans
200 years

Plastic bags
20 years

Milk carton
3 months

Cotton t-shirt
5 months

Apple core
2 months

Banana peel
5 weeks

Slow to decompose

Fast to decompose

Science to the rescue

Scientists are working hard to find new materials that decompose in faster and healthier ways, as well as trying to figure out how to repair and rebuild reefs.

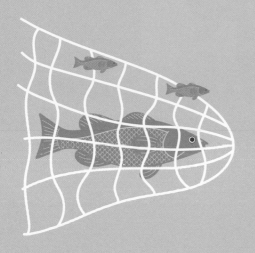

Sustainable fishing

New biodegradable fishing nets are being developed. They have larger holes so small fish can escape and be given a chance to grow and have their own babies.

Attracting back fish

After discovering that noisy reefs are healthy reefs, scientists have developed speakers that can play fish sounds underwater. These can be placed at restored reef sites to attract fish back.

Coral gardens

Scientists noticed that corals could grow on other materials after seeing them grow over shipwrecks. They used this idea to grow coral gardens from small samples of corals which they hang in the sea.

Protected areas

More marine reserves are being established to protect areas from being harmed by motor boats and overfishing. Limiting the number of visitors also reduces plastic garbage in the areas.

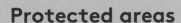

GLOSSARY

BIODEGRADABLE—a material or object that can break down into smaller pieces over time.

BIODIVERSITY—the variety of plant and animal life on Earth or in a particular habitat.

BIOLUMINESCENCE—the production of light by a living organism through chemical reactions.

ENDANGERED—an animal or plant that is dying out and soon may not exist anymore.

FOOD CHAIN—the order in which animals depend on each other for food.

INVERTEBRATE—an animal that doesn't have a backbone.

NOCTURNAL—an animal that moves around and feeds at night.

PREDATOR—an animal that hunts and kills other animals for food.

PREY—an animal that is hunted or caught by other animals for food.

SUSTAINABLE—using resources in a way that ensures they will continue to be available.

SYMBIOSIS—a close relationship between two different types of organisms or living things.

VERTEBRATE—an animal that has a backbone.

INDEX

ABOUT THE AUTHOR

Vassiliki Tzomaka is a designer and illustrator based in Colchester, UK. She has a PhD in Children's Book Illustration from the Cambridge School of Art and an MEnv in Environmental Studies from the University of Essex. She is the author of *Hoot and Howl across the Desert* (2020), also published by Thames & Hudson.

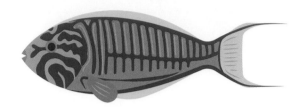

Designed by Emily Sear

Marine Consultancy by Olivia Forster

First published in 2021 in the United States of America by Thames & Hudson Inc., 500 Fifth Avenue, New York, New York 10110

Library of Congress Control Number 2020951868

ISBN 978-0-500-65231-2

Printed and bound in China by Leo Paper Products Ltd.

MIX
Paper from responsible sources
FSC® C020056

Be the first to know about our new releases, exclusive content and author events by visiting
thamesandhudson.com
thamesandhudsonusa.com
thamesandhudson.com.au